How to Art Doodle Color Patterns

Carolyn Scrace

This edition first published in MMXV by
Book House

Distributed by Black Rabbit Books
P.O. Box 3263
Mankato
Minnesota MN 56002

© MMXV The Salariya Book Company Ltd
Printed in the United States of America.
Printed on paper from sustainable forests.

Cataloging-in-Publication Data is available
from the Library of Congress

HB ISBN: 978-1-909645-47-9
PB ISBN: 978-1-910184-33-2

How to Art Doodle™

Color Patterns

BOOK HOUSE

Carolyn Scrace

Contents

Please note: Sharp blades and scissors should be used under adult supervision.

Introduction

Art Doodling stimulates creativity and develops drawing skills. Discover the thrill of using simple, color Art Doodle patterns to build up a complex picture. These pages are packed with inspirational ideas and designs and show how easy it is to achieve these incredible effects.

Do it anywhere!

Art Doodling can be done anywhere, and needs no special equipment! Some of the best Art Doodles are often drawn on the backs of envelopes or paper towels!

Inspiration

Just look at the colors and patterns in front of you right now for inspiration! Before long you will start to see ideas for Art Doodle patterns and color combinations everywhere—even in the most suprising places!

Sketchbook

Keep a small sketchbook or notepad with you at all times. Use it like a scrap book: collect any interesting cuttings, photos, and snippets of fabric and stick them in. Jot down notes and make sketches of anything you find visually exciting.

Color combinations

Color can build atmosphere or create a mood in a picture. Certain color combinations will attract attention. Learn about color temperatures and different coloring techniques.

Color wheel

Art Doodle your own color wheel and use it as a color guide when creating artwork.

1. Use compasses to draw two concentric circles. Divide the circle shape into twelve equal sections (see below).

2. Draw a triangle in the center and divide it in three. Add three small triangles (see below).

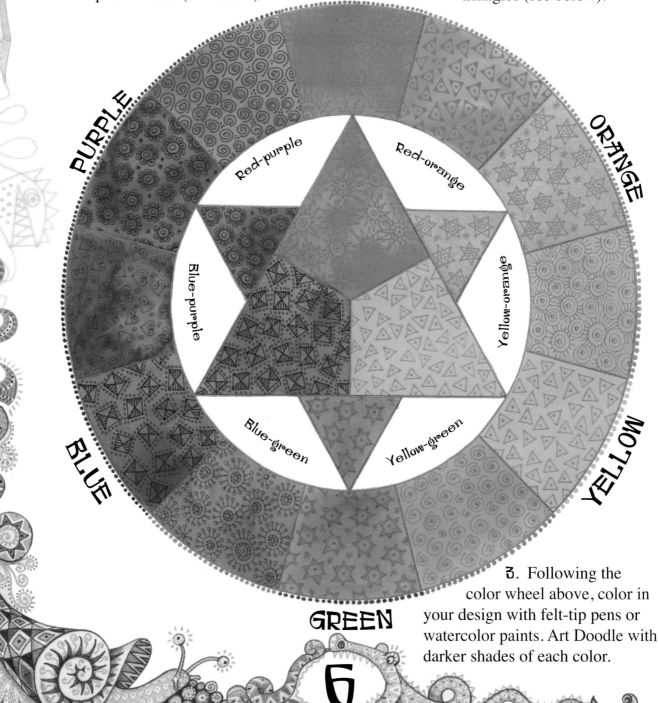

RED

ORANGE

YELLOW

GREEN

BLUE

PURPLE

Red-purple

Red-orange

Blue-purple

Yellow-orange

Blue-green

Yellow-green

3. Following the color wheel above, color in your design with felt-tip pens or watercolor paints. Art Doodle with darker shades of each color.

6

Primary colors

The primary colors (red, yellow, and blue) are the three colors of pigment that cannot be mixed from any other colors. All other colors are derived from these three primaries.

Secondary colors

Green, orange, and purple are called secondary colors. They are each formed by mixing two of the primary colors.

Tertiary colors

The six tertiary colors are created by mixing a primary and a secondary color. They are red-orange, red-purple, blue-purple, blue-green, yellow-green, and yellow-orange.

Complementary colors

Colors that lie on opposite sides of the color wheel (p 6) are called complementary colors. For example red and green clash when used together, creating a vibrant, contrasting color scheme.

Analogous colors

Colors that lie adjacent to each other on the color wheel (p 6) are called analogous colors. They produce harmonious color schemes, for example blue and purple, red and orange.

Pencil sharpener

Graphite pencils come in different grades, from hard to soft. The softer the pencil, the darker the mark it makes.

Eraser

Thick-tipped marker pens are perfect for filling in large areas. Fine-tipped, permanent marker pens are great for outlines and adding detail.

Tools & materials

There are no special tools and materials needed for Art Doodling. An old pencil stub and a scrap of paper are all you need to get started! You may, however, wish to use some or all of the tools and materials suggested here. It's important to experiment and try to use whatever tools and materials inspire and excite you.

Pencil crayons are ideal for adding soft shading to an area. Use them for coloring in.

Felt-tip pens come in a range of thicknesses. Thick pens are ideal for blocking-in large areas of color.

Fineliner pens produce a flowing line. They come in a wide range of colors and are ideal for intricate doodling.

A **black gel pen** is useful for outlines and detailed doodles. **Metallic** and **white gel pens** are ideal for doodling onto colored paper or over dark-colored Art Doodles.

8

Ruler

Compasses are used for drawing circles and arcs. (Alternatively, cups and saucers make an ideal substitute.)

Types of paper

Cartridge paper comes in a variety of weights. Heavyweight paper is good for water-based paint. Note: Ink lines may bleed on some cartridge paper.

Bristol board or **paper** may be textured or smooth. **Smooth Bristol board** is good to work on with pencils, pencil crayons, markers, felt-tips, and gel and fineliner pens for adding fine details.

Colored inks and **watercolor paints** are ideal for covering large areas of a design with subtle color. Use them to create exciting backgrounds for Art Doodles (see pages 20-21).

Gouache is opaque watercolor. Use it for painting areas with plain, flat color.

Sketchbook for jotting down ideas and trying out designs.

Use your sketchbook for experimenting with new techniques and keep notes of what materials you used.

Palette (or clean saucer) for mixing paint.

Paintbrushes come in a wide range of sizes.

Color schemes

Monochrome color schemes use different shades of one single color. Choose a color from the color wheel and see how many variations you can achieve by changing the tonal value and adding Art Doodles.

1. Use compasses to draw a circle. Divide it into 12 equal parts.

2. Use watercolors to paint each part a different shade of blue.

3. Art Doodle the design in felt-tips, fineliner, or gel pens. White and silver gel pens are ideal for adding pale patterns over darker areas.

10

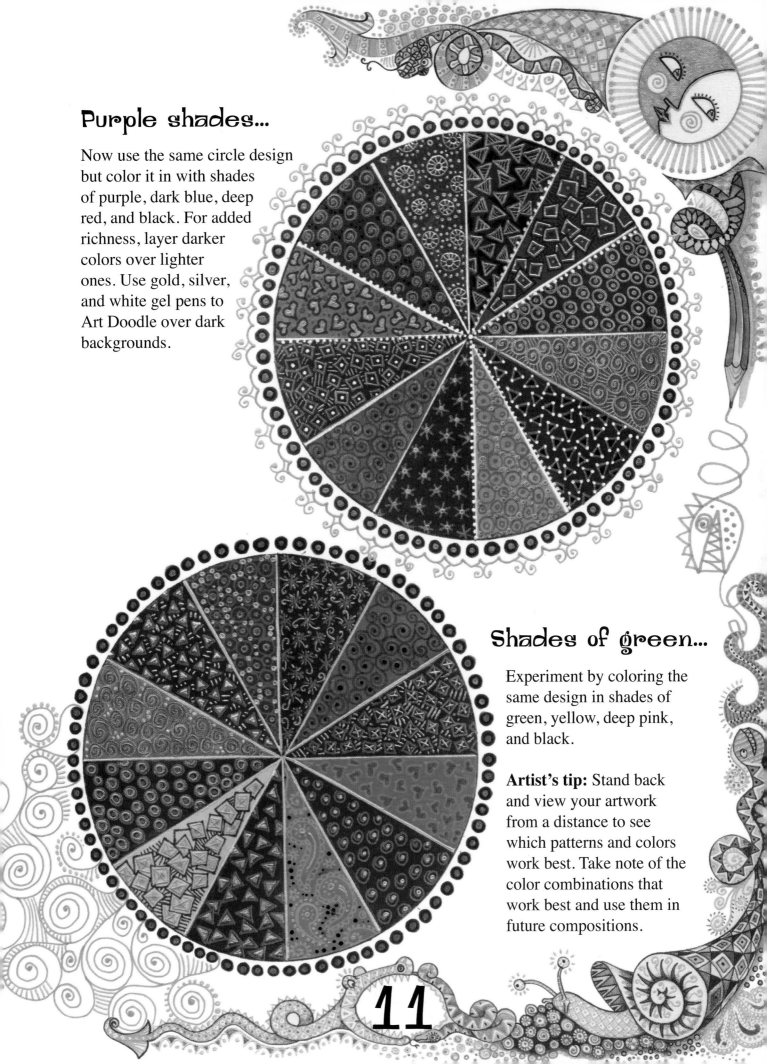

Purple shades...

Now use the same circle design but color it in with shades of purple, dark blue, deep red, and black. For added richness, layer darker colors over lighter ones. Use gold, silver, and white gel pens to Art Doodle over dark backgrounds.

Shades of green...

Experiment by coloring the same design in shades of green, yellow, deep pink, and black.

Artist's tip: Stand back and view your artwork from a distance to see which patterns and colors work best. Take note of the color combinations that work best and use them in future compositions.

11

Limited palette

When artists use a limited palette it means they are using a restricted number of colors to create designs. Turn to the color wheel (p 6) and select just a few colors to use for your Art Doodle.

Analogous colors are used in this design: yellow, yellow-orange, orange, and green.

Additionally, darker shades of these colors, and black and white complete the palette.

Taking a line for a walk...

1. Blind doodling is an easy, fun way to create an Art Doodle composition! You need a sheet of paper, a pen or pencil—then simply close your eyes and take the line for a walk! Don't peep and don't take your hand off the paper.

2. The blind-doodled line will create random, exciting shapes. Use black gel or fineliner pen to draw in some Art Doodle patterns. Turn to the Pattern Builder (p 22) for step-by-step guides to create some amazing doodles.

3. Using the limited palette you chose earlier, color in the Art Doodles with felt-tip, fineliner, and gel pens.

4. An analogous color scheme produces harmonious combinations and sophisticated results. Contrasting areas of black and white add impact to the overall design.

Rainbow colors

The colors of the rainbow are red, orange, yellow, green, blue, indigo, and violet. Red lies at the top of a rainbow and violet at the bottom.

1. First draw a rough thumbnail sketch of your design on scrap paper. (These strange shapes were created by drawing around random ink blots).

2. Once you are happy with your design, redraw it on a large sheet of paper. Add more lines and shapes to create a structure for the doodles.

3. Add repeat bands of rainbow colors across the design. Use felt-tip pens, pencil crayons, or watercolor paint to add color.

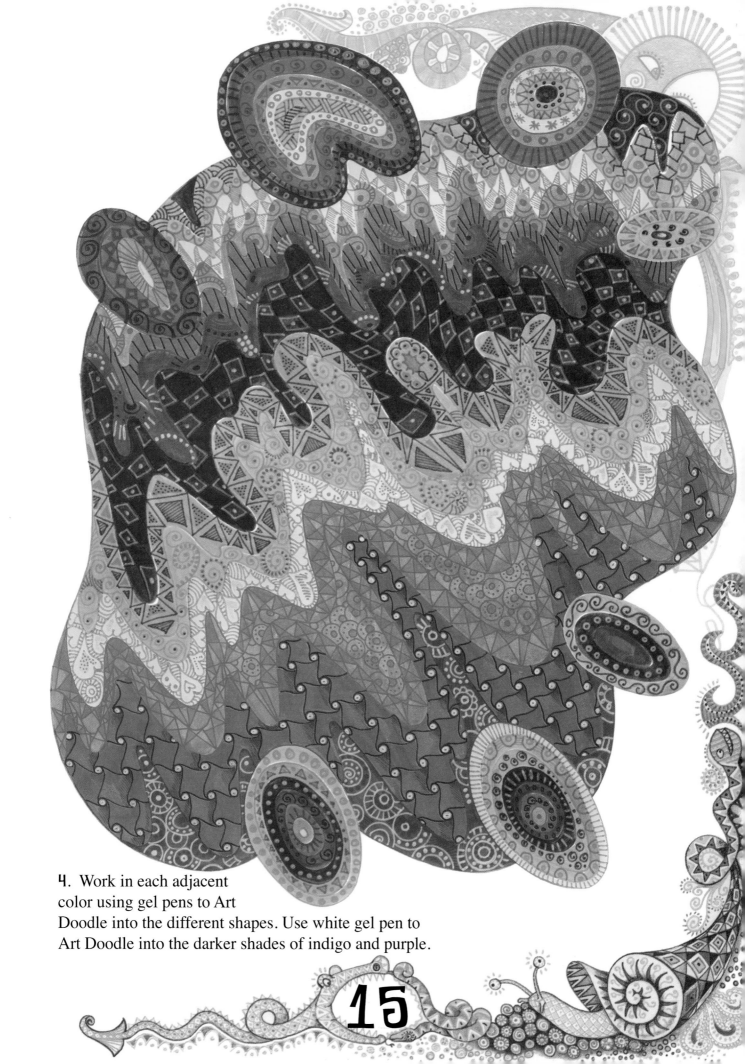

4. Work in each adjacent
color using gel pens to Art
Doodle into the different shapes. Use white gel pen to
Art Doodle into the darker shades of indigo and purple.

15

Inspiration

The artist Wassily Kandinsky was a pioneer of abstract art. He felt that painting didn't need to be realistic, but that abstract shape and color alone could express great emotion. He likened the emotional impact of shape and color to the joy of listening to beautiful music.

1. Sketch in a rough design inspired by Kandinsky's stunning compositions. Using felt-tip pens, try out some of Kandinsky's clashing color schemes.

2. Draw out your finished Art Doodle design. Use watercolor paints and felt-tip pens to fill in blocks of color. Experiment by using fluorescent yellow, green, pink, and blue highlighters as base colors!

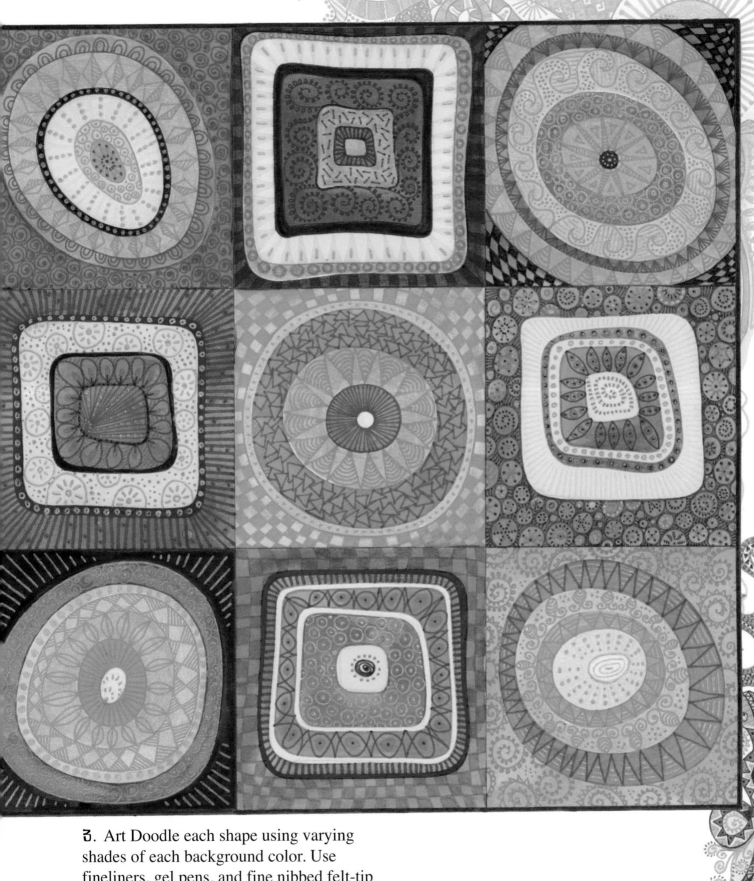

3. Art Doodle each shape using varying shades of each background color. Use fineliners, gel pens, and fine nibbed felt-tip pens. Draw in a thin black frame to finish off your eye-catching design.

17

Temperature

Color temperature refers to the warmth or coolness of color. For example reds, oranges, and yellows—the colors of the sun and fire—are known as warm colors. Blues, greens and purples—the colors of the seas and landscape—are cool colors.

Sun and moon

1. Sketch in a rough design based on the shape of a crescent moon overlapping the sun's face. Construct a series of concentric circles as the basis for your composition. Color in your rough using warm colors for the sun's side of the image and cool colors on the moon's side.

2. Pencil in the finished design on cartridge paper. Go over the pencil lines using water-resistant black fineliner. Begin blocking-in large areas using watercolor paints.

3. Contrasting areas of light and dark tone give impact to the design. Using black Art Doodles on top of a color is an easy method of creating a darker tone. White gel pen doodles will lighten an area of color.

4. Use gold and silver gel pens to doodle on top of dark reds and blues. Use alternating stripes of blue and turquoise around the moon's border.

Color temperatures reflect emotional qualities. Warm colors promote happiness and energy, while cool colors are associated with calmness and tranquility.

Random colors

The most exciting and creative effects can be achieved by using watercolor paints or ink washes. Simply drip random blobs of color onto a sheet of wet watercolor paper, then watch them run and bleed together into surprising combinations! The resulting subtle colors and unexpected shapes make superb backgrounds for Art Doodling.

1. Using a clean sponge, wet a thick sheet of watercolor or cartridge paper. Dab off any puddles of water, then drip watercolor paint onto the wet paper. Leave to dry completely.

2. Study the paint shapes now created as the basis for your Art Doodling. An irregular watermark shape can develop into a flower or doodle around tiny paint splats.

3. Black, white, or gold gel pens are ideal for Art Doodling onto brightly colored backgrounds.

Pattern builder

These step-by-step examples show how to Art Doodle some of the patterns used in this book.

Limited palette (pages 12-13)

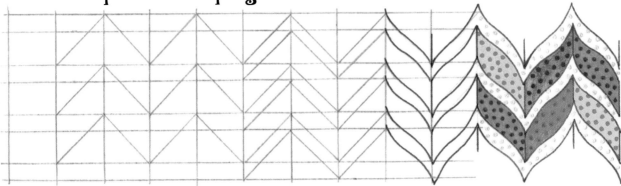

1. Draw a pencil grid (see above). Add rows of zigzag lines.

2. Add another set of zigzag lines below the first.

3. Ink in curved lines along each zigzag, then color in.

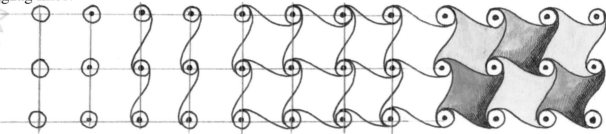

1. Draw a pencil grid. Ink in a dotted circle where the lines cross.

2. Link the circles vertically (as shown) using curved lines.

3. Repeat the curved lines horizontally. Now add color and shading.

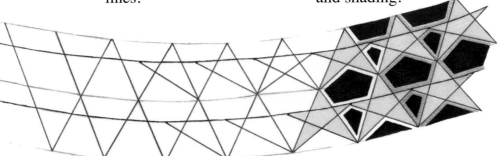

1. Pencil in curved, parallel lines (as shown). Draw zigzag lines that cross over.

2. Take an angled line from the base of each zigzag to the center of the line above.

3. Draw another line (as shown) to make a star shape. Color in the pattern.

Glossary

Abstract art   a painting or sculpture that does not depict a person, place, or thing.

Analogous colors   harmonious colors that lie next to each other on the color wheel (page 6).

Background   area behind an object or image.

Color temperatures   the coolness or warmth of a color (blue-green is coldest and red-orange is warmest).

Color wheel   a circular diagram in which primary and tertiary colors are arranged so that related colors are next to each other and complementary colors are opposite.

Compasses   instrument for drawing circles and arcs.

Complementary colors   colors that lie on opposite sides of the color wheel (p 6).

Composition   how an artist arranges shapes, sizes, and colors, the different elements that make a piece of art.

Design   a graphic representation, usually a drawing or a sketch.

Harmonious colors   a pleasing arrangement of colors.

Limited palette   when an artist restricts the number of colors used.

Monochrome   the use of different shades and tones of only one color.

Primary colors   the three colors (red, yellow, and blue) from which all other colors can be mixed.

Rough   a quick sketch of the main elements in a picture.

Secondary colors   the colors that are made by mixing the three primary colors.

Sketch   a preparatory drawing.

Technique   an accepted method used to produce something.

Tertiary colors   the colors formed by mixing a primary and a secondary color.

Thumbnail (sketches)   usually very small, quick, abbreviated drawings.

Index